Camping Jou

CAMP   MATCHES

I'D RATHER BE ROASTING MARSHMALLOWS

THIS CAMPING JOURNAL BELONGS TO

_____

TRIP #	CAMPGROUND NAME	STATE	PAGE #
1			6
2			8
3			10
4			12
5			14
6			16
7			18
8			20
9			22
10			24
11			26
12			28
13			30
14			32
15			34
16			36
17			38
18			40
19			42
20			44
21			46
22			48
23			50
24			52
25			54

TRIP #	CAMPGROUND NAME	STATE	PAGE #
26			56
27			58
28			60
29			62
30			64
31			66
32			68
33			70
34			72
35			74
36			76
37			78
38			80
39			82
40			84
41			86
42			88
43			90
44			92
45			94
46			96
47			98
48			100
49			102
50			104

1  CAMPGROUND INFORMATION

CAMPGROUND:_____ DATES:_____

LOCATION:_____ SITE #:_____

PHONE:_____ NIGHTLY RATE:_____

RESERVATION #:_____

CHECK IN TIME:_____ CHECK OUT TIME:_____

POSSIBLE SITES FOR NEXT VISIT:_____

CAMPGROUND RATING: 1 2 3 4 5 6 7 8 9 10

OTHER CAMPGROUNDS IN AREA   PHONE NUMBER

_____   _____

_____   _____

☐ WATER	☐ WIFI	☐ LAKE
☐ ELECTRIC	☐ CABLE TV	☐ BEACH ACCESS
☐ SEWER	☐ POOL	☐ NATURE TRAILS
☐ TENTS OK	☐ HOT TUB	☐ CAMP STORE
☐ PULL-THROUGH	☐ PATIO	☐ FITNESS ROOM
MAX TRAILER	☐ GRILL/BBQ	☐ RESTAURANT
LENGTH_____	☐ FIRE PIT	☐ VOLLEYBALL COURT
☐ DUMP STATION	☐ SHADY TREES	☐ MINI GOLF
☐ SHOWERS	☐ PICNIC TABLES	☐ PLAYGROUND
☐ LAUNDRY	☐ BIKE RENTAL	☐ CLUB HOUSE

OTHER AMMENITIES:_____

_____

CAMP

TRIP MEMORIES

WEATHER REPORT

What I Enjoyed Most:_____

_____

_____

_____

Most Memorable Event:_____

_____

_____

_____

Who I Camped With: _____

_____

People I Met: _____

_____

Places I Went: _____

_____

Things I Did: _____

_____

Things I Still Want To Try Or Do Next Time:_____

_____

_____

2  CAMPGROUND INFORMATION

CAMPGROUND:_____ DATES:_____

LOCATION:_____ SITE #:_____

PHONE:_____ NIGHTLY RATE:_____

RESERVATION #:_____

CHECK IN TIME:_____ CHECK OUT TIME:_____

POSSIBLE SITES FOR NEXT VISIT:_____

CAMPGROUND RATING: 1 2 3 4 5 6 7 8 9 10

OTHER CAMPGROUNDS IN AREA   PHONE NUMBER

_____   _____

_____   _____

☐ WATER	☐ WIFI	☐ LAKE
☐ ELECTRIC	☐ CABLE TV	☐ BEACH ACCESS
☐ SEWER	☐ POOL	☐ NATURE TRAILS
☐ TENTS OK	☐ HOT TUB	☐ CAMP STORE
☐ PULL-THROUGH	☐ PATIO	☐ FITNESS ROOM
MAX TRAILER	☐ GRILL/BBQ	☐ RESTAURANT
LENGTH_____	☐ FIRE PIT	☐ VOLLEYBALL COURT
☐ DUMP STATION	☐ SHADY TREES	☐ MINI GOLF
☐ SHOWERS	☐ PICNIC TABLES	☐ PLAYGROUND
☐ LAUNDRY	☐ BIKE RENTAL	☐ CLUB HOUSE

OTHER AMMENITIES:_____

_____

 CAMP

TRIP MEMORIES

WEATHER REPORT

What I Enjoyed Most:_____

_____

_____

_____

Most Memorable Event:_____

_____

_____

_____

Who I Camped With: _____

_____

People I Met: _____

_____

Places I Went: _____

_____

Things I Did: _____

_____

Things I Still Want To Try Or Do Next Time:_____

_____

_____

3 CAMPGROUND INFORMATION

CAMPGROUND:_____ DATES:_____

LOCATION:_____ SITE #:_____

PHONE:_____ NIGHTLY RATE:_____

RESERVATION #:_____

CHECK IN TIME:_____ CHECK OUT TIME:_____

POSSIBLE SITES FOR NEXT VISIT:_____

CAMPGROUND RATING: 1 2 3 4 5 6 7 8 9 10

OTHER CAMPGROUNDS IN AREA   PHONE NUMBER

_____   _____

_____   _____

☐ WATER	☐ WIFI	☐ LAKE
☐ ELECTRIC	☐ CABLE TV	☐ BEACH ACCESS
☐ SEWER	☐ POOL	☐ NATURE TRAILS
☐ TENTS OK	☐ HOT TUB	☐ CAMP STORE
☐ PULL-THROUGH	☐ PATIO	☐ FITNESS ROOM
MAX TRAILER	☐ GRILL/BBQ	☐ RESTAURANT
LENGTH_____	☐ FIRE PIT	☐ VOLLEYBALL COURT
☐ DUMP STATION	☐ SHADY TREES	☐ MINI GOLF
☐ SHOWERS	☐ PICNIC TABLES	☐ PLAYGROUND
☐ LAUNDRY	☐ BIKE RENTAL	☐ CLUB HOUSE

OTHER AMMENITIES:_____

_____

 CAMP

TRIP MEMORIES

WEATHER REPORT

What I Enjoyed Most:_____
_____
_____
_____

Most Memorable Event:_____
_____
_____
_____

Who I Camped With: _____
_____

People I Met: _____
_____

Places I Went: _____
_____

Things I Did: _____
_____

Things I Still Want To Try Or Do Next Time:_____
_____
_____

4  CAMPGROUND INFORMATION

CAMPGROUND:_____ DATES:_____

LOCATION:_____ SITE #:_____

PHONE:_____ NIGHTLY RATE:_____

RESERVATION #:_____

CHECK IN TIME:_____ CHECK OUT TIME:_____

POSSIBLE SITES FOR NEXT VISIT:_____

CAMPGROUND RATING: 1 2 3 4 5 6 7 8 9 10

OTHER CAMPGROUNDS IN AREA   PHONE NUMBER

_____   _____

_____   _____

☐ WATER	☐ WIFI	☐ LAKE
☐ ELECTRIC	☐ CABLE TV	☐ BEACH ACCESS
☐ SEWER	☐ POOL	☐ NATURE TRAILS
☐ TENTS OK	☐ HOT TUB	☐ CAMP STORE
☐ PULL-THROUGH	☐ PATIO	☐ FITNESS ROOM
MAX TRAILER	☐ GRILL/BBQ	☐ RESTAURANT
LENGTH_____	☐ FIRE PIT	☐ VOLLEYBALL COURT
☐ DUMP STATION	☐ SHADY TREES	☐ MINI GOLF
☐ SHOWERS	☐ PICNIC TABLES	☐ PLAYGROUND
☐ LAUNDRY	☐ BIKE RENTAL	☐ CLUB HOUSE

OTHER AMMENITIES:_____

_____

TRIP MEMORIES

WEATHER REPORT

What I Enjoyed Most:_____

_____

_____

_____

Most Memorable Event:_____

_____

_____

_____

Who I Camped With: _____

_____

People I Met: _____

_____

Places I Went: _____

_____

Things I Did: _____

_____

Things I Still Want To Try Or Do Next Time:_____

_____

_____

5  CAMPGROUND INFORMATION

CAMPGROUND:_____ DATES:_____

LOCATION:_____ SITE #:_____

PHONE:_____ NIGHTLY RATE:_____

RESERVATION #:_____

CHECK IN TIME:_____ CHECK OUT TIME:_____

POSSIBLE SITES FOR NEXT VISIT:_____

CAMPGROUND RATING: 1 2 3 4 5 6 7 8 9 10

OTHER CAMPGROUNDS IN AREA   PHONE NUMBER

_____   _____

_____   _____

☐ WATER	☐ WIFI	☐ LAKE
☐ ELECTRIC	☐ CABLE TV	☐ BEACH ACCESS
☐ SEWER	☐ POOL	☐ NATURE TRAILS
☐ TENTS OK	☐ HOT TUB	☐ CAMP STORE
☐ PULL-THROUGH	☐ PATIO	☐ FITNESS ROOM
MAX TRAILER	☐ GRILL/BBQ	☐ RESTAURANT
LENGTH_____	☐ FIRE PIT	☐ VOLLEYBALL COURT
☐ DUMP STATION	☐ SHADY TREES	☐ MINI GOLF
☐ SHOWERS	☐ PICNIC TABLES	☐ PLAYGROUND
☐ LAUNDRY	☐ BIKE RENTAL	☐ CLUB HOUSE

OTHER AMMENITIES:_____

_____

 **CAMP**

TRIP MEMORIES

WEATHER REPORT

What I Enjoyed Most:_____

_____

_____

_____

Most Memorable Event:_____

_____

_____

_____

Who I Camped With: _____

_____

People I Met: _____

_____

Places I Went: _____

_____

Things I Did: _____

_____

Things I Still Want To Try Or Do Next Time:_____

_____

_____

6  CAMPGROUND INFORMATION

CAMPGROUND:_____ DATES:_____

LOCATION:_____ SITE #:_____

PHONE:_____ NIGHTLY RATE:_____

RESERVATION #:_____

CHECK IN TIME:_____ CHECK OUT TIME:_____

POSSIBLE SITES FOR NEXT VISIT:_____

CAMPGROUND RATING: 1   2   3   4   5   6   7   8   9   10

OTHER CAMPGROUNDS IN AREA   PHONE NUMBER

_____   _____

_____   _____

□ WATER	□ WIFI	□ LAKE
□ ELECTRIC	□ CABLE TV	□ BEACH ACCESS
□ SEWER	□ POOL	□ NATURE TRAILS
□ TENTS OK	□ HOT TUB	□ CAMP STORE
□ PULL-THROUGH	□ PATIO	□ FITNESS ROOM
MAX TRAILER	□ GRILL/BBQ	□ RESTAURANT
LENGTH_____	□ FIRE PIT	□ VOLLEYBALL COURT
□ DUMP STATION	□ SHADY TREES	□ MINI GOLF
□ SHOWERS	□ PICNIC TABLES	□ PLAYGROUND
□ LAUNDRY	□ BIKE RENTAL	□ CLUB HOUSE

OTHER AMMENITIES:_____

_____

TRIP MEMORIES

WEATHER REPORT

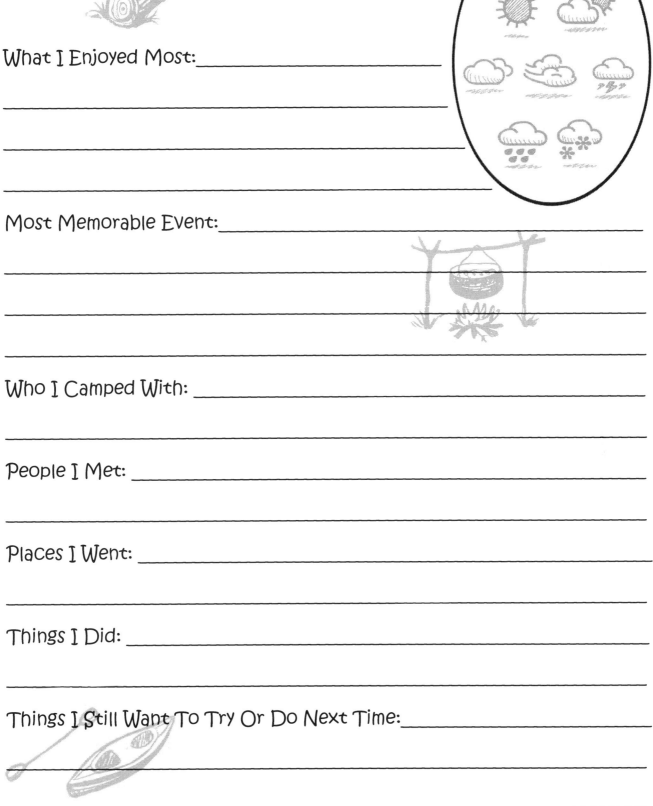

What I Enjoyed Most: _____

_____

_____

Most Memorable Event: _____

_____

_____

_____

Who I Camped With: _____

_____

People I Met: _____

_____

Places I Went: _____

_____

Things I Did: _____

_____

Things I Still Want To Try Or Do Next Time: _____

_____

_____

7  CAMPGROUND INFORMATION

CAMPGROUND:_____ DATES:_____

LOCATION:_____ SITE #:_____

PHONE:_____ NIGHTLY RATE:_____

RESERVATION #:_____

CHECK IN TIME:_____ CHECK OUT TIME:_____

POSSIBLE SITES FOR NEXT VISIT:_____

CAMPGROUND RATING: 1 2 3 4 5 6 7 8 9 10

OTHER CAMPGROUNDS IN AREA   PHONE NUMBER

_____   _____

_____   _____

☐ WATER	☐ WIFI	☐ LAKE
☐ ELECTRIC	☐ CABLE TV	☐ BEACH ACCESS
☐ SEWER	☐ POOL	☐ NATURE TRAILS
☐ TENTS OK	☐ HOT TUB	☐ CAMP STORE
☐ PULL-THROUGH	☐ PATIO	☐ FITNESS ROOM
MAX TRAILER	☐ GRILL/BBQ	☐ RESTAURANT
LENGTH_____	☐ FIRE PIT	☐ VOLLEYBALL COURT
☐ DUMP STATION	☐ SHADY TREES	☐ MINI GOLF
☐ SHOWERS	☐ PICNIC TABLES	☐ PLAYGROUND
☐ LAUNDRY	☐ BIKE RENTAL	☐ CLUB HOUSE

OTHER AMMENITIES:_____

_____

CAMP

TRIP MEMORIES

WEATHER REPORT

What I Enjoyed Most:_____

_____

_____

_____

Most Memorable Event:_____

_____

_____

_____

Who I Camped With: _____

_____

People I Met: _____

_____

Places I Went: _____

_____

Things I Did: _____

_____

Things I Still Want To Try Or Do Next Time:_____

_____

_____

8 CAMPGROUND INFORMATION

CAMPGROUND:_____ DATES:_____

LOCATION:_____ SITE #:_____

PHONE:_____ NIGHTLY RATE:_____

RESERVATION #:_____

CHECK IN TIME:_____ CHECK OUT TIME:_____

POSSIBLE SITES FOR NEXT VISIT:_____

CAMPGROUND RATING: 1 2 3 4 5 6 7 8 9 10

OTHER CAMPGROUNDS IN AREA   PHONE NUMBER

_____   _____

_____   _____

☐ WATER	☐ WIFI	☐ LAKE
☐ ELECTRIC	☐ CABLE TV	☐ BEACH ACCESS
☐ SEWER	☐ POOL	☐ NATURE TRAILS
☐ TENTS OK	☐ HOT TUB	☐ CAMP STORE
☐ PULL-THROUGH	☐ PATIO	☐ FITNESS ROOM
MAX TRAILER LENGTH_____	☐ GRILL/BBQ	☐ RESTAURANT
	☐ FIRE PIT	☐ VOLLEYBALL COURT
☐ DUMP STATION	☐ SHADY TREES	☐ MINI GOLF
☐ SHOWERS	☐ PICNIC TABLES	☐ PLAYGROUND
☐ LAUNDRY	☐ BIKE RENTAL	☐ CLUB HOUSE

OTHER AMMENITIES:_____

_____

 CAMP

TRIP MEMORIES

WEATHER REPORT

What I Enjoyed Most:_____

_____

_____

_____

Most Memorable Event:_____

_____

_____

_____

Who I Camped With: _____

_____

People I Met: _____

_____

Places I Went: _____

_____

Things I Did: _____

_____

Things I Still Want To Try Or Do Next Time:_____

_____

_____

9 CAMPGROUND INFORMATION

CAMPGROUND:_____ DATES:_____

LOCATION:_____ SITE #:_____

PHONE:_____ NIGHTLY RATE:_____

RESERVATION #:_____

CHECK IN TIME:_____ CHECK OUT TIME:_____

POSSIBLE SITES FOR NEXT VISIT:_____

CAMPGROUND RATING: 1 2 3 4 5 6 7 8 9 10

OTHER CAMPGROUNDS IN AREA   PHONE NUMBER

_____   _____

_____   _____

□ WATER	□ WIFI	□ LAKE
□ ELECTRIC	□ CABLE TV	□ BEACH ACCESS
□ SEWER	□ POOL	□ NATURE TRAILS
□ TENTS OK	□ HOT TUB	□ CAMP STORE
□ PULL-THROUGH	□ PATIO	□ FITNESS ROOM
MAX TRAILER	□ GRILL/BBQ	□ RESTAURANT
LENGTH_____	□ FIRE PIT	□ VOLLEYBALL COURT
□ DUMP STATION	□ SHADY TREES	□ MINI GOLF
□ SHOWERS	□ PICNIC TABLES	□ PLAYGROUND
□ LAUNDRY	□ BIKE RENTAL	□ CLUB HOUSE

OTHER AMMENITIES:_____

_____

 # TRIP MEMORIES

WEATHER REPORT

What I Enjoyed Most:_____

_____

_____

_____

Most Memorable Event:_____

_____

_____

_____

Who I Camped With: _____

_____

People I Met: _____

_____

Places I Went: _____

_____

Things I Did: _____

_____

Things I Still Want To Try Or Do Next Time:_____

_____

_____

10 CAMPGROUND INFORMATION

CAMPGROUND:_____ DATES:_____

LOCATION:_____ SITE #:_____

PHONE:_____ NIGHTLY RATE:_____

RESERVATION #:_____

CHECK IN TIME:_____ CHECK OUT TIME:_____

POSSIBLE SITES FOR NEXT VISIT:_____

CAMPGROUND RATING: 1 2 3 4 5 6 7 8 9 10

OTHER CAMPGROUNDS IN AREA   PHONE NUMBER

_____   _____

_____   _____

☐ WATER	☐ WIFI	☐ LAKE
☐ ELECTRIC	☐ CABLE TV	☐ BEACH ACCESS
☐ SEWER	☐ POOL	☐ NATURE TRAILS
☐ TENTS OK	☐ HOT TUB	☐ CAMP STORE
☐ PULL-THROUGH	☐ PATIO	☐ FITNESS ROOM
MAX TRAILER	☐ GRILL/BBQ	☐ RESTAURANT
LENGTH_____	☐ FIRE PIT	☐ VOLLEYBALL COURT
☐ DUMP STATION	☐ SHADY TREES	☐ MINI GOLF
☐ SHOWERS	☐ PICNIC TABLES	☐ PLAYGROUND
☐ LAUNDRY	☐ BIKE RENTAL	☐ CLUB HOUSE

OTHER AMMENITIES:_____

_____

 **CAMP**

TRIP MEMORIES

WEATHER REPORT

What I Enjoyed Most:_____

_____

_____

_____

Most Memorable Event:_____

_____

_____

_____

Who I Camped With: _____

_____

People I Met: _____

_____

Places I Went: _____

_____

Things I Did: _____

_____

Things I Still Want To Try Or Do Next Time:_____

_____

_____

11 CAMPGROUND INFORMATION

CAMPGROUND:_____ DATES:_____

LOCATION:_____ SITE #:_____

PHONE:_____ NIGHTLY RATE:_____

RESERVATION #:_____

CHECK IN TIME:_____ CHECK OUT TIME:_____

POSSIBLE SITES FOR NEXT VISIT:_____

CAMPGROUND RATING: 1 2 3 4 5 6 7 8 9 10

OTHER CAMPGROUNDS IN AREA   PHONE NUMBER

_____   _____

_____   _____

☐ WATER	☐ WIFI	☐ LAKE
☐ ELECTRIC	☐ CABLE TV	☐ BEACH ACCESS
☐ SEWER	☐ POOL	☐ NATURE TRAILS
☐ TENTS OK	☐ HOT TUB	☐ CAMP STORE
☐ PULL-THROUGH	☐ PATIO	☐ FITNESS ROOM
MAX TRAILER	☐ GRILL/BBQ	☐ RESTAURANT
LENGTH_____	☐ FIRE PIT	☐ VOLLEYBALL COURT
☐ DUMP STATION	☐ SHADY TREES	☐ MINI GOLF
☐ SHOWERS	☐ PICNIC TABLES	☐ PLAYGROUND
☐ LAUNDRY	☐ BIKE RENTAL	☐ CLUB HOUSE

OTHER AMMENITIES:_____

_____

CAMP

TRIP MEMORIES

WEATHER REPORT

What I Enjoyed Most:_____

_____

_____

_____

Most Memorable Event:_____

_____

_____

_____

Who I Camped With: _____

_____

People I Met: _____

_____

Places I Went: _____

_____

Things I Did: _____

_____

Things I Still Want To Try Or Do Next Time:_____

_____

_____

12 CAMPGROUND INFORMATION

CAMPGROUND:_____ DATES:_____

LOCATION:_____ SITE #:_____

PHONE:_____ NIGHTLY RATE:_____

RESERVATION #:_____

CHECK IN TIME:_____ CHECK OUT TIME:_____

POSSIBLE SITES FOR NEXT VISIT:_____

CAMPGROUND RATING: 1   2   3   4   5   6   7   8   9   10

OTHER CAMPGROUNDS IN AREA   PHONE NUMBER

_____   _____

_____   _____

☐ WATER	☐ WIFI	☐ LAKE
☐ ELECTRIC	☐ CABLE TV	☐ BEACH ACCESS
☐ SEWER	☐ POOL	☐ NATURE TRAILS
☐ TENTS OK	☐ HOT TUB	☐ CAMP STORE
☐ PULL-THROUGH	☐ PATIO	☐ FITNESS ROOM
MAX TRAILER	☐ GRILL/BBQ	☐ RESTAURANT
LENGTH_____	☐ FIRE PIT	☐ VOLLEYBALL COURT
☐ DUMP STATION	☐ SHADY TREES	☐ MINI GOLF
☐ SHOWERS	☐ PICNIC TABLES	☐ PLAYGROUND
☐ LAUNDRY	☐ BIKE RENTAL	☐ CLUB HOUSE

OTHER AMMENITIES:_____

_____

 CAMP

TRIP MEMORIES

WEATHER REPORT

What I Enjoyed Most:_____

_____

_____

_____

Most Memorable Event:_____

_____

_____

_____

Who I Camped With: _____

_____

People I Met: _____

_____

Places I Went: _____

_____

Things I Did: _____

_____

Things I Still Want To Try Or Do Next Time:_____

_____

_____

13 CAMPGROUND INFORMATION

CAMPGROUND:_____ DATES:_____

LOCATION:_____ SITE #:_____

PHONE:_____ NIGHTLY RATE:_____

RESERVATION #:_____

CHECK IN TIME:_____ CHECK OUT TIME:_____

POSSIBLE SITES FOR NEXT VISIT:_____

CAMPGROUND RATING: 1 2 3 4 5 6 7 8 9 10

OTHER CAMPGROUNDS IN AREA   PHONE NUMBER

_____   _____

_____   _____

☐ WATER	☐ WIFI	☐ LAKE
☐ ELECTRIC	☐ CABLE TV	☐ BEACH ACCESS
☐ SEWER	☐ POOL	☐ NATURE TRAILS
☐ TENTS OK	☐ HOT TUB	☐ CAMP STORE
☐ PULL-THROUGH	☐ PATIO	☐ FITNESS ROOM
MAX TRAILER	☐ GRILL/BBQ	☐ RESTAURANT
LENGTH_____	☐ FIRE PIT	☐ VOLLEYBALL COURT
☐ DUMP STATION	☐ SHADY TREES	☐ MINI GOLF
☐ SHOWERS	☐ PICNIC TABLES	☐ PLAYGROUND
☐ LAUNDRY	☐ BIKE RENTAL	☐ CLUB HOUSE

OTHER AMMENITIES:_____

_____

CAMP

TRIP MEMORIES

WEATHER REPORT

What I Enjoyed Most:_____

_____

_____

Most Memorable Event:_____

_____

_____

Who I Camped With: _____

_____

People I Met: _____

_____

Places I Went: _____

_____

Things I Did: _____

_____

Things I Still Want To Try Or Do Next Time:_____

_____

_____

14  CAMPGROUND INFORMATION

CAMPGROUND:_____ DATES:_____

LOCATION:_____ SITE #:_____

PHONE:_____ NIGHTLY RATE:_____

RESERVATION #:_____

CHECK IN TIME:_____ CHECK OUT TIME:_____

POSSIBLE SITES FOR NEXT VISIT:_____

CAMPGROUND RATING: 1   2   3   4   5   6   7   8   9   10

OTHER CAMPGROUNDS IN AREA   PHONE NUMBER

_____   _____

_____   _____

☐ WATER	☐ WIFI	☐ LAKE
☐ ELECTRIC	☐ CABLE TV	☐ BEACH ACCESS
☐ SEWER	☐ POOL	☐ NATURE TRAILS
☐ TENTS OK	☐ HOT TUB	☐ CAMP STORE
☐ PULL-THROUGH	☐ PATIO	☐ FITNESS ROOM
MAX TRAILER	☐ GRILL/BBQ	☐ RESTAURANT
LENGTH_____	☐ FIRE PIT	☐ VOLLEYBALL COURT
☐ DUMP STATION	☐ SHADY TREES	☐ MINI GOLF
☐ SHOWERS	☐ PICNIC TABLES	☐ PLAYGROUND
☐ LAUNDRY	☐ BIKE RENTAL	☐ CLUB HOUSE

OTHER AMMENITIES:_____

_____

 # TRIP MEMORIES

WEATHER REPORT

What I Enjoyed Most:_____

_____

_____

_____

Most Memorable Event:_____

_____

_____

_____

Who I Camped With: _____

_____

People I Met: _____

_____

Places I Went: _____

_____

Things I Did: _____

_____

Things I Still Want To Try Or Do Next Time:_____

_____

_____

15 CAMPGROUND INFORMATION

CAMPGROUND:_____ DATES:_____

LOCATION:_____ SITE #:_____

PHONE:_____ NIGHTLY RATE:_____

RESERVATION #:_____

CHECK IN TIME:_____ CHECK OUT TIME:_____

POSSIBLE SITES FOR NEXT VISIT:_____

CAMPGROUND RATING: 1   2   3   4   5   6   7   8   9   10

OTHER CAMPGROUNDS IN AREA   PHONE NUMBER

_____   _____

_____   _____

☐ WATER	☐ WIFI	☐ LAKE
☐ ELECTRIC	☐ CABLE TV	☐ BEACH ACCESS
☐ SEWER	☐ POOL	☐ NATURE TRAILS
☐ TENTS OK	☐ HOT TUB	☐ CAMP STORE
☐ PULL-THROUGH	☐ PATIO	☐ FITNESS ROOM
MAX TRAILER	☐ GRILL/BBQ	☐ RESTAURANT
LENGTH_____	☐ FIRE PIT	☐ VOLLEYBALL COURT
☐ DUMP STATION	☐ SHADY TREES	☐ MINI GOLF
☐ SHOWERS	☐ PICNIC TABLES	☐ PLAYGROUND
☐ LAUNDRY	☐ BIKE RENTAL	☐ CLUB HOUSE

OTHER AMMENITIES:_____

_____

TRIP MEMORIES

WEATHER REPORT

What I Enjoyed Most:_____

_____

_____

_____

Most Memorable Event:_____

_____

_____

_____

Who I Camped With: _____

_____

People I Met: _____

_____

Places I Went: _____

_____

Things I Did: _____

_____

Things I Still Want To Try Or Do Next Time:_____

_____

_____

16 CAMPGROUND INFORMATION

CAMPGROUND:_____ DATES:_____

LOCATION:_____ SITE #:_____

PHONE:_____ NIGHTLY RATE:_____

RESERVATION #:_____

CHECK IN TIME:_____ CHECK OUT TIME:_____

POSSIBLE SITES FOR NEXT VISIT:_____

CAMPGROUND RATING: 1 2 3 4 5 6 7 8 9 10

OTHER CAMPGROUNDS IN AREA   PHONE NUMBER

_____   _____

_____   _____

☐ WATER	☐ WIFI	☐ LAKE
☐ ELECTRIC	☐ CABLE TV	☐ BEACH ACCESS
☐ SEWER	☐ POOL	☐ NATURE TRAILS
☐ TENTS OK	☐ HOT TUB	☐ CAMP STORE
☐ PULL-THROUGH	☐ PATIO	☐ FITNESS ROOM
MAX TRAILER	☐ GRILL/BBQ	☐ RESTAURANT
LENGTH_____	☐ FIRE PIT	☐ VOLLEYBALL COURT
☐ DUMP STATION	☐ SHADY TREES	☐ MINI GOLF
☐ SHOWERS	☐ PICNIC TABLES	☐ PLAYGROUND
☐ LAUNDRY	☐ BIKE RENTAL	☐ CLUB HOUSE

OTHER AMMENITIES:_____

_____

TRIP MEMORIES

WEATHER REPORT

What I Enjoyed Most:_____

_____

_____

_____

Most Memorable Event:_____

_____

_____

_____

Who I Camped With: _____

_____

People I Met: _____

_____

Places I Went: _____

_____

Things I Did: _____

_____

Things I Still Want To Try Or Do Next Time:_____

_____

_____

17 CAMPGROUND INFORMATION

CAMPGROUND:_____ DATES:_____

LOCATION:_____ SITE #:_____

PHONE:_____ NIGHTLY RATE:_____

RESERVATION #:_____

CHECK IN TIME:_____ CHECK OUT TIME:_____

POSSIBLE SITES FOR NEXT VISIT:_____

CAMPGROUND RATING: 1   2   3   4   5   6   7   8   9   10

OTHER CAMPGROUNDS IN AREA   PHONE NUMBER

_____   _____

_____   _____

WATER	WIFI	LAKE
☐ WATER	☐ WIFI	☐ LAKE
☐ ELECTRIC	☐ CABLE TV	☐ BEACH ACCESS
☐ SEWER	☐ POOL	☐ NATURE TRAILS
☐ TENTS OK	☐ HOT TUB	☐ CAMP STORE
☐ PULL-THROUGH	☐ PATIO	☐ FITNESS ROOM
MAX TRAILER	☐ GRILL/BBQ	☐ RESTAURANT
LENGTH_____	☐ FIRE PIT	☐ VOLLEYBALL COURT
☐ DUMP STATION	☐ SHADY TREES	☐ MINI GOLF
☐ SHOWERS	☐ PICNIC TABLES	☐ PLAYGROUND
☐ LAUNDRY	☐ BIKE RENTAL	☐ CLUB HOUSE

OTHER AMMENITIES:_____

_____

 **CAMP**

TRIP MEMORIES

WEATHER REPORT

What I Enjoyed Most:_____

_____

_____

Most Memorable Event:_____

_____

_____

_____

Who I Camped With: _____

_____

People I Met: _____

_____

Places I Went: _____

_____

Things I Did: _____

_____

Things I Still Want To Try Or Do Next Time:_____

_____

_____

18 CAMPGROUND INFORMATION

CAMPGROUND:_____ DATES:_____

LOCATION:_____ SITE #:_____

PHONE:_____ NIGHTLY RATE:_____

RESERVATION #:_____

CHECK IN TIME:_____ CHECK OUT TIME:_____

POSSIBLE SITES FOR NEXT VISIT:_____

CAMPGROUND RATING: 1 2 3 4 5 6 7 8 9 10

OTHER CAMPGROUNDS IN AREA   PHONE NUMBER

_____   _____

_____   _____

☐ WATER	☐ WIFI	☐ LAKE
☐ ELECTRIC	☐ CABLE TV	☐ BEACH ACCESS
☐ SEWER	☐ POOL	☐ NATURE TRAILS
☐ TENTS OK	☐ HOT TUB	☐ CAMP STORE
☐ PULL-THROUGH	☐ PATIO	☐ FITNESS ROOM
MAX TRAILER	☐ GRILL/BBQ	☐ RESTAURANT
LENGTH_____	☐ FIRE PIT	☐ VOLLEYBALL COURT
☐ DUMP STATION	☐ SHADY TREES	☐ MINI GOLF
☐ SHOWERS	☐ PICNIC TABLES	☐ PLAYGROUND
☐ LAUNDRY	☐ BIKE RENTAL	☐ CLUB HOUSE

OTHER AMMENITIES:_____

_____

TRIP MEMORIES

WEATHER REPORT

What I Enjoyed Most:_____

_____

_____

_____

Most Memorable Event:_____

_____

_____

_____

Who I Camped With: _____

_____

People I Met: _____

_____

Places I Went: _____

_____

Things I Did: _____

_____

Things I Still Want To Try Or Do Next Time:_____

_____

_____

19 CAMPGROUND INFORMATION

CAMPGROUND:_____ DATES:_____

LOCATION:_____ SITE #:_____

PHONE:_____ NIGHTLY RATE:_____

RESERVATION #:_____

CHECK IN TIME:_____ CHECK OUT TIME:_____

POSSIBLE SITES FOR NEXT VISIT:_____

CAMPGROUND RATING: 1 2 3 4 5 6 7 8 9 10

OTHER CAMPGROUNDS IN AREA   PHONE NUMBER

_____   _____

_____   _____

☐ WATER	☐ WIFI	☐ LAKE
☐ ELECTRIC	☐ CABLE TV	☐ BEACH ACCESS
☐ SEWER	☐ POOL	☐ NATURE TRAILS
☐ TENTS OK	☐ HOT TUB	☐ CAMP STORE
☐ PULL-THROUGH	☐ PATIO	☐ FITNESS ROOM
MAX TRAILER	☐ GRILL/BBQ	☐ RESTAURANT
LENGTH_____	☐ FIRE PIT	☐ VOLLEYBALL COURT
☐ DUMP STATION	☐ SHADY TREES	☐ MINI GOLF
☐ SHOWERS	☐ PICNIC TABLES	☐ PLAYGROUND
☐ LAUNDRY	☐ BIKE RENTAL	☐ CLUB HOUSE

OTHER AMMENITIES:_____

_____

 **TRIP MEMORIES**

WEATHER REPORT

What I Enjoyed Most:_____

_____

_____

_____

Most Memorable Event:_____

_____

_____

_____

Who I Camped With: _____

_____

People I Met: _____

_____

Places I Went: _____

_____

Things I Did: _____

_____

Things I Still Want To Try Or Do Next Time:_____

_____

_____

20  CAMPGROUND INFORMATION

CAMPGROUND:_____ DATES:_____

LOCATION:_____ SITE #:_____

PHONE:_____ NIGHTLY RATE:_____

RESERVATION #:_____

CHECK IN TIME:_____ CHECK OUT TIME:_____

POSSIBLE SITES FOR NEXT VISIT:_____

CAMPGROUND RATING:　　1　2　3　4　5　6　7　8　9　10

OTHER CAMPGROUNDS IN AREA　　　PHONE NUMBER

_____　　_____

_____　　_____

☐ WATER	☐ WIFI	☐ LAKE
☐ ELECTRIC	☐ CABLE TV	☐ BEACH ACCESS
☐ SEWER	☐ POOL	☐ NATURE TRAILS
☐ TENTS OK	☐ HOT TUB	☐ CAMP STORE
☐ PULL-THROUGH	☐ PATIO	☐ FITNESS ROOM
MAX TRAILER	☐ GRILL/BBQ	☐ RESTAURANT
LENGTH_____	☐ FIRE PIT	☐ VOLLEYBALL COURT
☐ DUMP STATION	☐ SHADY TREES	☐ MINI GOLF
☐ SHOWERS	☐ PICNIC TABLES	☐ PLAYGROUND
☐ LAUNDRY	☐ BIKE RENTAL	☐ CLUB HOUSE

OTHER AMMENITIES:_____

_____

TRIP MEMORIES

WEATHER REPORT

What I Enjoyed Most:_____

_____

_____

_____

Most Memorable Event:_____

_____

_____

_____

Who I Camped With: _____

_____

People I Met: _____

_____

Places I Went: _____

_____

Things I Did: _____

_____

Things I Still Want To Try Or Do Next Time:_____

_____

21 CAMPGROUND INFORMATION

CAMPGROUND:_____ DATES:_____

LOCATION:_____ SITE #:_____

PHONE:_____ NIGHTLY RATE:_____

RESERVATION #:_____

CHECK IN TIME:_____ CHECK OUT TIME:_____

POSSIBLE SITES FOR NEXT VISIT:_____

CAMPGROUND RATING: 1 2 3 4 5 6 7 8 9 10

OTHER CAMPGROUNDS IN AREA   PHONE NUMBER

_____   _____

_____   _____

☐ WATER	☐ WIFI	☐ LAKE
☐ ELECTRIC	☐ CABLE TV	☐ BEACH ACCESS
☐ SEWER	☐ POOL	☐ NATURE TRAILS
☐ TENTS OK	☐ HOT TUB	☐ CAMP STORE
☐ PULL-THROUGH	☐ PATIO	☐ FITNESS ROOM
MAX TRAILER	☐ GRILL/BBQ	☐ RESTAURANT
LENGTH_____	☐ FIRE PIT	☐ VOLLEYBALL COURT
☐ DUMP STATION	☐ SHADY TREES	☐ MINI GOLF
☐ SHOWERS	☐ PICNIC TABLES	☐ PLAYGROUND
☐ LAUNDRY	☐ BIKE RENTAL	☐ CLUB HOUSE

OTHER AMMENITIES:_____

_____

 CAMP

TRIP MEMORIES

WEATHER REPORT

What I Enjoyed Most:_____

_____

_____

Most Memorable Event:_____

_____

_____

_____

Who I Camped With: _____

_____

People I Met: _____

_____

Places I Went: _____

_____

Things I Did: _____

_____

Things I Still Want To Try Or Do Next Time:_____

_____

_____

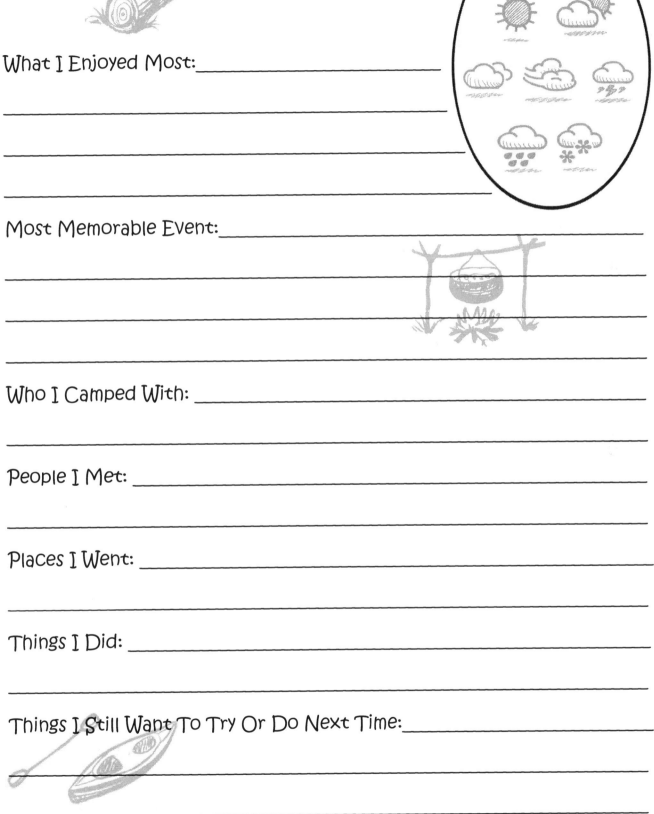

22  CAMPGROUND INFORMATION

CAMPGROUND:_____ DATES:_____

LOCATION:_____ SITE #:_____

PHONE:_____ NIGHTLY RATE:_____

RESERVATION #:_____

CHECK IN TIME:_____ CHECK OUT TIME:_____

POSSIBLE SITES FOR NEXT VISIT:_____

CAMPGROUND RATING: 1 2 3 4 5 6 7 8 9 10

OTHER CAMPGROUNDS IN AREA   PHONE NUMBER

_____   _____

_____   _____

☐ WATER	☐ WIFI	☐ LAKE
☐ ELECTRIC	☐ CABLE TV	☐ BEACH ACCESS
☐ SEWER	☐ POOL	☐ NATURE TRAILS
☐ TENTS OK	☐ HOT TUB	☐ CAMP STORE
☐ PULL-THROUGH	☐ PATIO	☐ FITNESS ROOM
MAX TRAILER	☐ GRILL/BBQ	☐ RESTAURANT
LENGTH_____	☐ FIRE PIT	☐ VOLLEYBALL COURT
☐ DUMP STATION	☐ SHADY TREES	☐ MINI GOLF
☐ SHOWERS	☐ PICNIC TABLES	☐ PLAYGROUND
☐ LAUNDRY	☐ BIKE RENTAL	☐ CLUB HOUSE

OTHER AMMENITIES:_____

_____

 **CAMP** **TRIP MEMORIES** WEATHER REPORT

What I Enjoyed Most:_____

_____

_____

_____

Most Memorable Event:_____

_____

_____

_____

Who I Camped With: _____

_____

People I Met: _____

_____

Places I Went: _____

_____

Things I Did: _____

_____

Things I Still Want To Try Or Do Next Time:_____

_____

_____

23  CAMPGROUND INFORMATION

CAMPGROUND:_____ DATES:_____

LOCATION:_____ SITE #:_____

PHONE:_____ NIGHTLY RATE:_____

RESERVATION #:_____

CHECK IN TIME:_____ CHECK OUT TIME:_____

POSSIBLE SITES FOR NEXT VISIT:_____

CAMPGROUND RATING: 1   2   3   4   5   6   7   8   9   10

OTHER CAMPGROUNDS IN AREA   PHONE NUMBER

_____   _____

_____   _____

☐ WATER	☐ WIFI	☐ LAKE
☐ ELECTRIC	☐ CABLE TV	☐ BEACH ACCESS
☐ SEWER	☐ POOL	☐ NATURE TRAILS
☐ TENTS OK	☐ HOT TUB	☐ CAMP STORE
☐ PULL-THROUGH	☐ PATIO	☐ FITNESS ROOM
MAX TRAILER	☐ GRILL/BBQ	☐ RESTAURANT
LENGTH_____	☐ FIRE PIT	☐ VOLLEYBALL COURT
☐ DUMP STATION	☐ SHADY TREES	☐ MINI GOLF
☐ SHOWERS	☐ PICNIC TABLES	☐ PLAYGROUND
☐ LAUNDRY	☐ BIKE RENTAL	☐ CLUB HOUSE

OTHER AMMENITIES:_____

_____

 **TRIP MEMORIES**

WEATHER REPORT

What I Enjoyed Most:_____

_____

_____

_____

Most Memorable Event:_____

_____

_____

_____

Who I Camped With: _____

_____

People I Met: _____

_____

Places I Went: _____

_____

Things I Did: _____

_____

Things I Still Want To Try Or Do Next Time:_____

_____

_____

24 CAMPGROUND INFORMATION

CAMPGROUND:_____ DATES:_____

LOCATION:_____ SITE #:_____

PHONE:_____ NIGHTLY RATE:_____

RESERVATION #:_____

CHECK IN TIME:_____ CHECK OUT TIME:_____

POSSIBLE SITES FOR NEXT VISIT:_____

CAMPGROUND RATING: 1   2   3   4   5   6   7   8   9   10

OTHER CAMPGROUNDS IN AREA   PHONE NUMBER

_____   _____

_____   _____

☐ WATER	☐ WIFI	☐ LAKE
☐ ELECTRIC	☐ CABLE TV	☐ BEACH ACCESS
☐ SEWER	☐ POOL	☐ NATURE TRAILS
☐ TENTS OK	☐ HOT TUB	☐ CAMP STORE
☐ PULL-THROUGH	☐ PATIO	☐ FITNESS ROOM
MAX TRAILER	☐ GRILL/BBQ	☐ RESTAURANT
LENGTH_____	☐ FIRE PIT	☐ VOLLEYBALL COURT
☐ DUMP STATION	☐ SHADY TREES	☐ MINI GOLF
☐ SHOWERS	☐ PICNIC TABLES	☐ PLAYGROUND
☐ LAUNDRY	☐ BIKE RENTAL	☐ CLUB HOUSE

OTHER AMMENITIES:_____

_____

 **CAMP**

TRIP MEMORIES

WEATHER REPORT

What I Enjoyed Most:_____

_____

_____

_____

Most Memorable Event:_____

_____

_____

_____

Who I Camped With: _____

_____

People I Met: _____

_____

Places I Went: _____

_____

Things I Did: _____

_____

Things I Still Want To Try Or Do Next Time:_____

_____

_____

25  CAMPGROUND INFORMATION

CAMPGROUND:_____ DATES:_____

LOCATION:_____ SITE #:_____

PHONE:_____ NIGHTLY RATE:_____

RESERVATION #:_____

CHECK IN TIME:_____ CHECK OUT TIME:_____

POSSIBLE SITES FOR NEXT VISIT:_____

CAMPGROUND RATING: 1   2   3   4   5   6   7   8   9   10

OTHER CAMPGROUNDS IN AREA   PHONE NUMBER

_____   _____

_____   _____

☐ WATER	☐ WIFI	☐ LAKE
☐ ELECTRIC	☐ CABLE TV	☐ BEACH ACCESS
☐ SEWER	☐ POOL	☐ NATURE TRAILS
☐ TENTS OK	☐ HOT TUB	☐ CAMP STORE
☐ PULL-THROUGH	☐ PATIO	☐ FITNESS ROOM
MAX TRAILER	☐ GRILL/BBQ	☐ RESTAURANT
LENGTH_____	☐ FIRE PIT	☐ VOLLEYBALL COURT
☐ DUMP STATION	☐ SHADY TREES	☐ MINI GOLF
☐ SHOWERS	☐ PICNIC TABLES	☐ PLAYGROUND
☐ LAUNDRY	☐ BIKE RENTAL	☐ CLUB HOUSE

OTHER AMMENITIES:_____

_____

 **CAMP**

TRIP MEMORIES

WEATHER REPORT

What I Enjoyed Most: _____

_____

_____

_____

Most Memorable Event: _____

_____

_____

_____

Who I Camped With: _____

_____

People I Met: _____

_____

Places I Went: _____

_____

Things I Did: _____

_____

Things I Still Want To Try Or Do Next Time: _____

_____

_____

26  CAMPGROUND INFORMATION

CAMPGROUND:_____ DATES:_____

LOCATION:_____ SITE #:_____

PHONE:_____ NIGHTLY RATE:_____

RESERVATION #:_____

CHECK IN TIME:_____ CHECK OUT TIME:_____

POSSIBLE SITES FOR NEXT VISIT:_____

CAMPGROUND RATING: 1 2 3 4 5 6 7 8 9 10

OTHER CAMPGROUNDS IN AREA   PHONE NUMBER

_____   _____

_____   _____

☐ WATER	☐ WIFI	☐ LAKE
☐ ELECTRIC	☐ CABLE TV	☐ BEACH ACCESS
☐ SEWER	☐ POOL	☐ NATURE TRAILS
☐ TENTS OK	☐ HOT TUB	☐ CAMP STORE
☐ PULL-THROUGH	☐ PATIO	☐ FITNESS ROOM
MAX TRAILER LENGTH_____	☐ GRILL/BBQ ☐ FIRE PIT	☐ RESTAURANT ☐ VOLLEYBALL COURT
☐ DUMP STATION	☐ SHADY TREES	☐ MINI GOLF
☐ SHOWERS	☐ PICNIC TABLES	☐ PLAYGROUND
☐ LAUNDRY	☐ BIKE RENTAL	☐ CLUB HOUSE

OTHER AMMENITIES:_____

_____

 **CAMP**   # TRIP MEMORIES

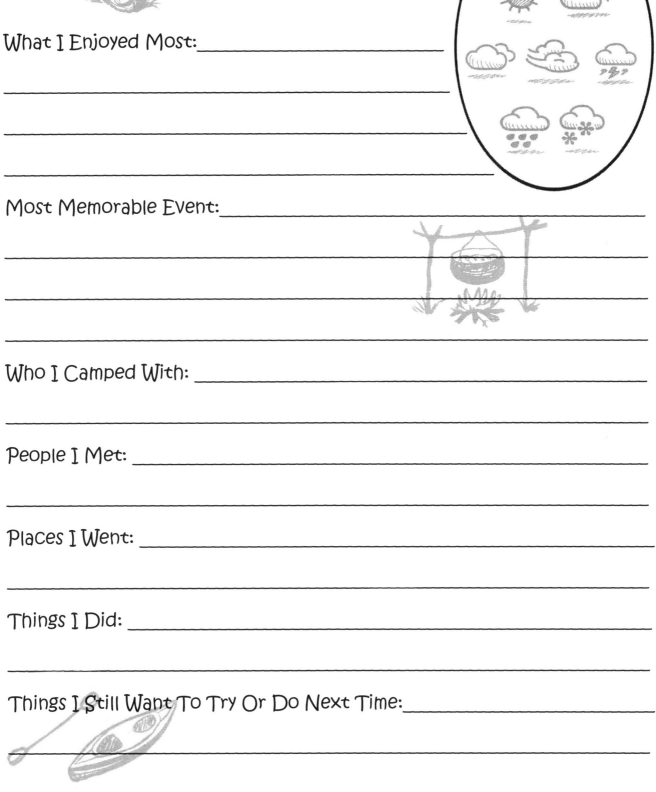

WEATHER REPORT

What I Enjoyed Most:_____

_____

_____

_____

Most Memorable Event:_____

_____

_____

_____

Who I Camped With: _____

_____

People I Met: _____

_____

Places I Went: _____

_____

Things I Did: _____

_____

Things I Still Want To Try Or Do Next Time:_____

_____

_____

27 CAMPGROUND INFORMATION

CAMPGROUND:_____ DATES:_____

LOCATION:_____ SITE #:_____

PHONE:_____ NIGHTLY RATE:_____

RESERVATION #:_____

CHECK IN TIME:_____ CHECK OUT TIME:_____

POSSIBLE SITES FOR NEXT VISIT:_____

CAMPGROUND RATING: 1 2 3 4 5 6 7 8 9 10

OTHER CAMPGROUNDS IN AREA   PHONE NUMBER

_____   _____

_____   _____

□ WATER	□ WIFI	□ LAKE
□ ELECTRIC	□ CABLE TV	□ BEACH ACCESS
□ SEWER	□ POOL	□ NATURE TRAILS
□ TENTS OK	□ HOT TUB	□ CAMP STORE
□ PULL-THROUGH	□ PATIO	□ FITNESS ROOM
MAX TRAILER	□ GRILL/BBQ	□ RESTAURANT
LENGTH_____	□ FIRE PIT	□ VOLLEYBALL COURT
□ DUMP STATION	□ SHADY TREES	□ MINI GOLF
□ SHOWERS	□ PICNIC TABLES	□ PLAYGROUND
□ LAUNDRY	□ BIKE RENTAL	□ CLUB HOUSE

OTHER AMMENITIES:_____

_____

 CAMP

TRIP MEMORIES

WEATHER REPORT

What I Enjoyed Most: _____

_____

_____

_____

Most Memorable Event: _____

_____

_____

_____

Who I Camped With: _____

_____

People I Met: _____

_____

Places I Went: _____

_____

Things I Did: _____

_____

Things I Still Want To Try Or Do Next Time: _____

_____

_____

28 CAMPGROUND INFORMATION

CAMPGROUND:_____ DATES:_____

LOCATION:_____ SITE #:_____

PHONE:_____ NIGHTLY RATE:_____

RESERVATION #:_____

CHECK IN TIME:_____ CHECK OUT TIME:_____

POSSIBLE SITES FOR NEXT VISIT:_____

CAMPGROUND RATING: 1 2 3 4 5 6 7 8 9 10

OTHER CAMPGROUNDS IN AREA   PHONE NUMBER

_____   _____

_____   _____

☐ WATER	☐ WIFI	☐ LAKE
☐ ELECTRIC	☐ CABLE TV	☐ BEACH ACCESS
☐ SEWER	☐ POOL	☐ NATURE TRAILS
☐ TENTS OK	☐ HOT TUB	☐ CAMP STORE
☐ PULL-THROUGH	☐ PATIO	☐ FITNESS ROOM
MAX TRAILER	☐ GRILL/BBQ	☐ RESTAURANT
LENGTH_____	☐ FIRE PIT	☐ VOLLEYBALL COURT
☐ DUMP STATION	☐ SHADY TREES	☐ MINI GOLF
☐ SHOWERS	☐ PICNIC TABLES	☐ PLAYGROUND
☐ LAUNDRY	☐ BIKE RENTAL	☐ CLUB HOUSE

OTHER AMMENITIES:_____

_____

 # CAMP

TRIP MEMORIES

WEATHER REPORT

What I Enjoyed Most:_____

_____

_____

_____

Most Memorable Event:_____

_____

_____

_____

Who I Camped With: _____

_____

People I Met: _____

_____

Places I Went: _____

_____

Things I Did: _____

_____

Things I Still Want To Try Or Do Next Time:_____

_____

_____

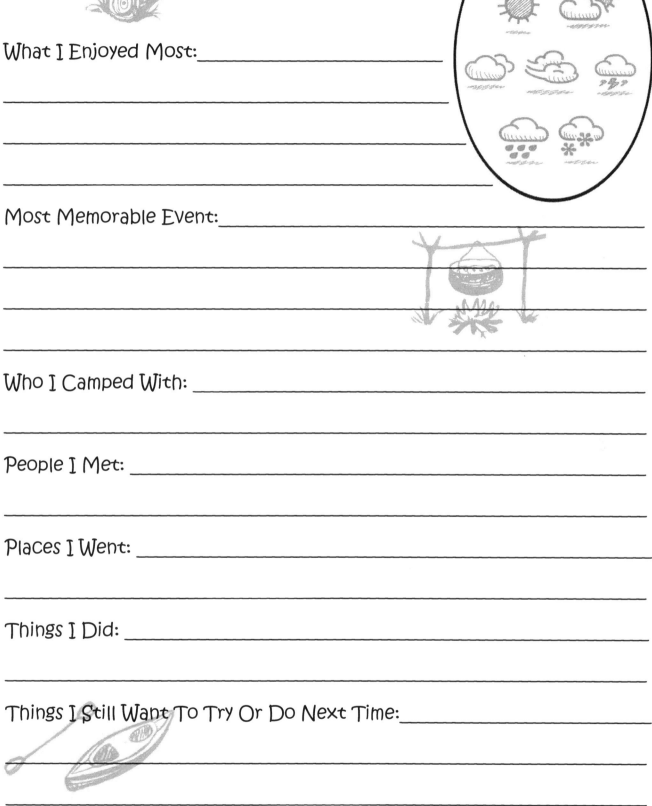

29  CAMPGROUND INFORMATION

CAMPGROUND:_____ DATES:_____

LOCATION:_____ SITE #:_____

PHONE:_____ NIGHTLY RATE:_____

RESERVATION #:_____

CHECK IN TIME:_____ CHECK OUT TIME:_____

POSSIBLE SITES FOR NEXT VISIT:_____

CAMPGROUND RATING: 1 2 3 4 5 6 7 8 9 10

OTHER CAMPGROUNDS IN AREA   PHONE NUMBER

_____   _____

_____   _____

☐ WATER	☐ WIFI	☐ LAKE
☐ ELECTRIC	☐ CABLE TV	☐ BEACH ACCESS
☐ SEWER	☐ POOL	☐ NATURE TRAILS
☐ TENTS OK	☐ HOT TUB	☐ CAMP STORE
☐ PULL-THROUGH	☐ PATIO	☐ FITNESS ROOM
MAX TRAILER	☐ GRILL/BBQ	☐ RESTAURANT
LENGTH_____	☐ FIRE PIT	☐ VOLLEYBALL COURT
☐ DUMP STATION	☐ SHADY TREES	☐ MINI GOLF
☐ SHOWERS	☐ PICNIC TABLES	☐ PLAYGROUND
☐ LAUNDRY	☐ BIKE RENTAL	☐ CLUB HOUSE

OTHER AMMENITIES:_____

_____

 **CAMP**

TRIP MEMORIES

WEATHER REPORT

What I Enjoyed Most:_____

_____

_____

_____

Most Memorable Event:_____

_____

_____

_____

Who I Camped With: _____

_____

People I Met: _____

_____

Places I Went: _____

_____

Things I Did: _____

_____

Things I Still Want To Try Or Do Next Time:_____

_____

_____

30 CAMPGROUND INFORMATION

CAMPGROUND:_____ DATES:_____

LOCATION:_____ SITE #:_____

PHONE:_____ NIGHTLY RATE:_____

RESERVATION #:_____

CHECK IN TIME:_____ CHECK OUT TIME:_____

POSSIBLE SITES FOR NEXT VISIT:_____

CAMPGROUND RATING: 1 2 3 4 5 6 7 8 9 10

OTHER CAMPGROUNDS IN AREA   PHONE NUMBER

_____   _____

_____   _____

□ WATER	□ WIFI	□ LAKE
□ ELECTRIC	□ CABLE TV	□ BEACH ACCESS
□ SEWER	□ POOL	□ NATURE TRAILS
□ TENTS OK	□ HOT TUB	□ CAMP STORE
□ PULL-THROUGH	□ PATIO	□ FITNESS ROOM
MAX TRAILER	□ GRILL/BBQ	□ RESTAURANT
LENGTH_____	□ FIRE PIT	□ VOLLEYBALL COURT
□ DUMP STATION	□ SHADY TREES	□ MINI GOLF
□ SHOWERS	□ PICNIC TABLES	□ PLAYGROUND
□ LAUNDRY	□ BIKE RENTAL	□ CLUB HOUSE

OTHER AMMENITIES:_____

_____

CAMP

TRIP MEMORIES

WEATHER REPORT

What I Enjoyed Most:_____

_____

_____

_____

Most Memorable Event:_____

_____

_____

_____

Who I Camped With: _____

_____

People I Met: _____

_____

Places I Went: _____

_____

Things I Did: _____

_____

Things I Still Want To Try Or Do Next Time:_____

_____

_____

31 CAMPGROUND INFORMATION

CAMPGROUND:_____ DATES:_____

LOCATION:_____ SITE #:_____

PHONE:_____ NIGHTLY RATE:_____

RESERVATION #:_____

CHECK IN TIME:_____ CHECK OUT TIME:_____

POSSIBLE SITES FOR NEXT VISIT:_____

CAMPGROUND RATING: 1   2   3   4   5   6   7   8   9   10

OTHER CAMPGROUNDS IN AREA   PHONE NUMBER

_____   _____

_____   _____

☐ WATER	☐ WIFI	☐ LAKE
☐ ELECTRIC	☐ CABLE TV	☐ BEACH ACCESS
☐ SEWER	☐ POOL	☐ NATURE TRAILS
☐ TENTS OK	☐ HOT TUB	☐ CAMP STORE
☐ PULL-THROUGH	☐ PATIO	☐ FITNESS ROOM
MAX TRAILER	☐ GRILL/BBQ	☐ RESTAURANT
LENGTH_____	☐ FIRE PIT	☐ VOLLEYBALL COURT
☐ DUMP STATION	☐ SHADY TREES	☐ MINI GOLF
☐ SHOWERS	☐ PICNIC TABLES	☐ PLAYGROUND
☐ LAUNDRY	☐ BIKE RENTAL	☐ CLUB HOUSE

OTHER AMMENITIES:_____

_____

 **CAMP**   # TRIP MEMORIES

WEATHER REPORT

What I Enjoyed Most:_____

_____

_____

_____

Most Memorable Event:_____

_____

_____

_____

Who I Camped With: _____

_____

People I Met: _____

_____

Places I Went: _____

_____

Things I Did: _____

_____

Things I Still Want To Try Or Do Next Time:_____

_____

_____

32 CAMPGROUND INFORMATION

CAMPGROUND:_____ DATES:_____

LOCATION:_____ SITE #:_____

PHONE:_____ NIGHTLY RATE:_____

RESERVATION #:_____

CHECK IN TIME:_____ CHECK OUT TIME:_____

POSSIBLE SITES FOR NEXT VISIT:_____

CAMPGROUND RATING: 1 2 3 4 5 6 7 8 9 10

OTHER CAMPGROUNDS IN AREA   PHONE NUMBER

_____   _____

_____   _____

☐ WATER	☐ WIFI	☐ LAKE
☐ ELECTRIC	☐ CABLE TV	☐ BEACH ACCESS
☐ SEWER	☐ POOL	☐ NATURE TRAILS
☐ TENTS OK	☐ HOT TUB	☐ CAMP STORE
☐ PULL-THROUGH	☐ PATIO	☐ FITNESS ROOM
MAX TRAILER	☐ GRILL/BBQ	☐ RESTAURANT
LENGTH_____	☐ FIRE PIT	☐ VOLLEYBALL COURT
☐ DUMP STATION	☐ SHADY TREES	☐ MINI GOLF
☐ SHOWERS	☐ PICNIC TABLES	☐ PLAYGROUND
☐ LAUNDRY	☐ BIKE RENTAL	☐ CLUB HOUSE

OTHER
AMMENITIES:_____

_____

 CAMP

TRIP MEMORIES

WEATHER REPORT

What I Enjoyed Most:_____

_____

_____

_____

Most Memorable Event:_____

_____

_____

_____

Who I Camped With: _____

_____

People I Met: _____

_____

Places I Went: _____

_____

Things I Did: _____

_____

Things I Still Want To Try Or Do Next Time:_____

_____

_____

33  CAMPGROUND INFORMATION

CAMPGROUND:_____ DATES:_____

LOCATION:_____ SITE #:_____

PHONE:_____ NIGHTLY RATE:_____

RESERVATION #:_____

CHECK IN TIME:_____ CHECK OUT TIME:_____

POSSIBLE SITES FOR NEXT VISIT:_____

CAMPGROUND RATING: 1 2 3 4 5 6 7 8 9 10

OTHER CAMPGROUNDS IN AREA   PHONE NUMBER

_____   _____

_____   _____

☐ WATER	☐ WIFI	☐ LAKE
☐ ELECTRIC	☐ CABLE TV	☐ BEACH ACCESS
☐ SEWER	☐ POOL	☐ NATURE TRAILS
☐ TENTS OK	☐ HOT TUB	☐ CAMP STORE
☐ PULL-THROUGH	☐ PATIO	☐ FITNESS ROOM
MAX TRAILER	☐ GRILL/BBQ	☐ RESTAURANT
LENGTH_____	☐ FIRE PIT	☐ VOLLEYBALL COURT
☐ DUMP STATION	☐ SHADY TREES	☐ MINI GOLF
☐ SHOWERS	☐ PICNIC TABLES	☐ PLAYGROUND
☐ LAUNDRY	☐ BIKE RENTAL	☐ CLUB HOUSE

OTHER AMMENITIES:_____

_____

 **CAMP**

TRIP MEMORIES

WEATHER REPORT

What I Enjoyed Most:_____

_____

_____

_____

Most Memorable Event:_____

_____

_____

_____

Who I Camped With: _____

_____

People I Met: _____

_____

Places I Went: _____

_____

Things I Did: _____

_____

Things I Still Want To Try Or Do Next Time:_____

_____

_____

34 CAMPGROUND INFORMATION

CAMPGROUND:_____ DATES:_____

LOCATION:_____ SITE #:_____

PHONE:_____ NIGHTLY RATE:_____

RESERVATION #:_____

CHECK IN TIME:_____ CHECK OUT TIME:_____

POSSIBLE SITES FOR NEXT VISIT:_____

CAMPGROUND RATING: 1   2   3   4   5   6   7   8   9   10

OTHER CAMPGROUNDS IN AREA   PHONE NUMBER

_____   _____

_____   _____

☐ WATER	☐ WIFI	☐ LAKE
☐ ELECTRIC	☐ CABLE TV	☐ BEACH ACCESS
☐ SEWER	☐ POOL	☐ NATURE TRAILS
☐ TENTS OK	☐ HOT TUB	☐ CAMP STORE
☐ PULL-THROUGH	☐ PATIO	☐ FITNESS ROOM
MAX TRAILER	☐ GRILL/BBQ	☐ RESTAURANT
LENGTH_____	☐ FIRE PIT	☐ VOLLEYBALL COURT
☐ DUMP STATION	☐ SHADY TREES	☐ MINI GOLF
☐ SHOWERS	☐ PICNIC TABLES	☐ PLAYGROUND
☐ LAUNDRY	☐ BIKE RENTAL	☐ CLUB HOUSE

OTHER AMMENITIES:_____

_____

 CAMP

TRIP MEMORIES

WEATHER REPORT

What I Enjoyed Most:_____

_____

_____

_____

Most Memorable Event:_____

_____

_____

_____

Who I Camped With: _____

_____

People I Met: _____

_____

Places I Went: _____

_____

Things I Did: _____

_____

Things I Still Want To Try Or Do Next Time:_____

_____

_____

35 CAMPGROUND INFORMATION

CAMPGROUND:_____ DATES:_____

LOCATION:_____ SITE #:_____

PHONE:_____ NIGHTLY RATE:_____

RESERVATION #:_____

CHECK IN TIME:_____ CHECK OUT TIME:_____

POSSIBLE SITES FOR NEXT VISIT:_____

CAMPGROUND RATING: 1 2 3 4 5 6 7 8 9 10

OTHER CAMPGROUNDS IN AREA   PHONE NUMBER

_____   _____

_____   _____

☐ WATER	☐ WIFI	☐ LAKE
☐ ELECTRIC	☐ CABLE TV	☐ BEACH ACCESS
☐ SEWER	☐ POOL	☐ NATURE TRAILS
☐ TENTS OK	☐ HOT TUB	☐ CAMP STORE
☐ PULL-THROUGH	☐ PATIO	☐ FITNESS ROOM
MAX TRAILER	☐ GRILL/BBQ	☐ RESTAURANT
LENGTH_____	☐ FIRE PIT	☐ VOLLEYBALL COURT
☐ DUMP STATION	☐ SHADY TREES	☐ MINI GOLF
☐ SHOWERS	☐ PICNIC TABLES	☐ PLAYGROUND
☐ LAUNDRY	☐ BIKE RENTAL	☐ CLUB HOUSE

OTHER AMMENITIES:_____

_____

 CAMP

TRIP MEMORIES

WEATHER REPORT

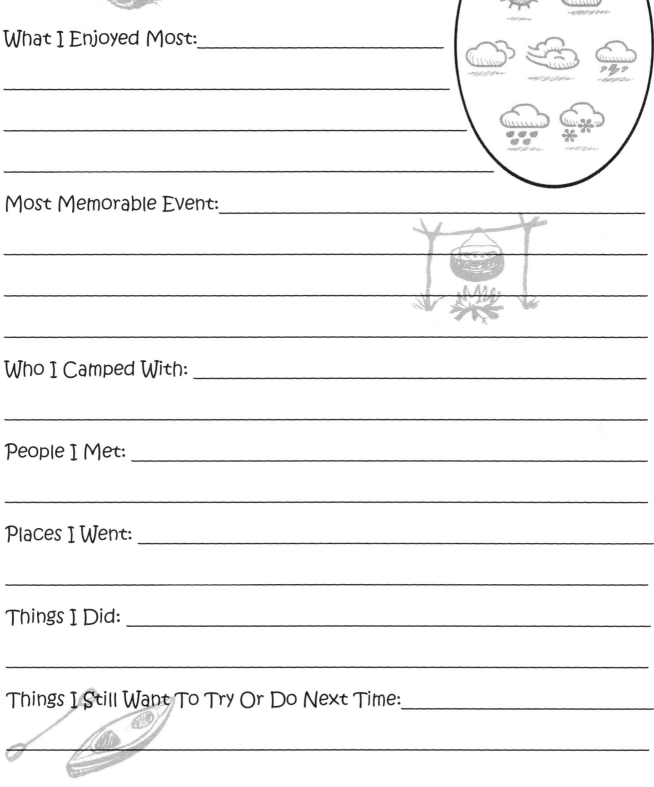

What I Enjoyed Most:_____

_____

_____

_____

Most Memorable Event:_____

_____

_____

_____

Who I Camped With: _____

_____

People I Met: _____

_____

Places I Went: _____

_____

Things I Did: _____

_____

Things I Still Want To Try Or Do Next Time:_____

_____

_____

36 CAMPGROUND INFORMATION

CAMPGROUND:_____ DATES:_____

LOCATION:_____ SITE #:_____

PHONE:_____ NIGHTLY RATE:_____

RESERVATION #:_____

CHECK IN TIME:_____ CHECK OUT TIME:_____

POSSIBLE SITES FOR NEXT VISIT:_____

CAMPGROUND RATING: 1 2 3 4 5 6 7 8 9 10

OTHER CAMPGROUNDS IN AREA   PHONE NUMBER

_____   _____

_____   _____

□ WATER	□ WIFI	□ LAKE
□ ELECTRIC	□ CABLE TV	□ BEACH ACCESS
□ SEWER	□ POOL	□ NATURE TRAILS
□ TENTS OK	□ HOT TUB	□ CAMP STORE
□ PULL-THROUGH	□ PATIO	□ FITNESS ROOM
MAX TRAILER	□ GRILL/BBQ	□ RESTAURANT
LENGTH_____	□ FIRE PIT	□ VOLLEYBALL COURT
□ DUMP STATION	□ SHADY TREES	□ MINI GOLF
□ SHOWERS	□ PICNIC TABLES	□ PLAYGROUND
□ LAUNDRY	□ BIKE RENTAL	□ CLUB HOUSE

OTHER AMMENITIES:_____

_____

 **CAMP**   # TRIP MEMORIES

WEATHER REPORT

What I Enjoyed Most:_____

_____

_____

_____

Most Memorable Event:_____

_____

_____

_____

Who I Camped With: _____

_____

People I Met: _____

_____

Places I Went: _____

_____

Things I Did: _____

_____

Things I Still Want To Try Or Do Next Time:_____

_____

_____

37 CAMPGROUND INFORMATION

CAMPGROUND:_____ DATES:_____

LOCATION:_____ SITE #:_____

PHONE:_____ NIGHTLY RATE:_____

RESERVATION #:_____

CHECK IN TIME:_____ CHECK OUT TIME:_____

POSSIBLE SITES FOR NEXT VISIT:_____

CAMPGROUND RATING: 1   2   3   4   5   6   7   8   9   10

OTHER CAMPGROUNDS IN AREA   PHONE NUMBER

_____   _____

☐ WATER	☐ WIFI	☐ LAKE
☐ ELECTRIC	☐ CABLE TV	☐ BEACH ACCESS
☐ SEWER	☐ POOL	☐ NATURE TRAILS
☐ TENTS OK	☐ HOT TUB	☐ CAMP STORE
☐ PULL-THROUGH	☐ PATIO	☐ FITNESS ROOM
MAX TRAILER	☐ GRILL/BBQ	☐ RESTAURANT
LENGTH_____	☐ FIRE PIT	☐ VOLLEYBALL COURT
☐ DUMP STATION	☐ SHADY TREES	☐ MINI GOLF
☐ SHOWERS	☐ PICNIC TABLES	☐ PLAYGROUND
☐ LAUNDRY	☐ BIKE RENTAL	☐ CLUB HOUSE

OTHER AMMENITIES:_____

_____

CAMP

TRIP MEMORIES

WEATHER REPORT

What I Enjoyed Most:_____

_____

_____

_____

Most Memorable Event:_____

_____

_____

_____

Who I Camped With: _____

_____

People I Met: _____

_____

Places I Went: _____

_____

Things I Did: _____

_____

Things I Still Want To Try Or Do Next Time:_____

_____

_____

38 CAMPGROUND INFORMATION

CAMPGROUND:_____ DATES:_____

LOCATION:_____ SITE #:_____

PHONE:_____ NIGHTLY RATE:_____

RESERVATION #:_____

CHECK IN TIME:_____ CHECK OUT TIME:_____

POSSIBLE SITES FOR NEXT VISIT:_____

CAMPGROUND RATING: 1   2   3   4   5   6   7   8   9   10

OTHER CAMPGROUNDS IN AREA   PHONE NUMBER

_____   _____

_____   _____

☐ WATER	☐ WIFI	☐ LAKE
☐ ELECTRIC	☐ CABLE TV	☐ BEACH ACCESS
☐ SEWER	☐ POOL	☐ NATURE TRAILS
☐ TENTS OK	☐ HOT TUB	☐ CAMP STORE
☐ PULL-THROUGH	☐ PATIO	☐ FITNESS ROOM
MAX TRAILER LENGTH_____	☐ GRILL/BBQ	☐ RESTAURANT
	☐ FIRE PIT	☐ VOLLEYBALL COURT
☐ DUMP STATION	☐ SHADY TREES	☐ MINI GOLF
☐ SHOWERS	☐ PICNIC TABLES	☐ PLAYGROUND
☐ LAUNDRY	☐ BIKE RENTAL	☐ CLUB HOUSE

OTHER AMMENITIES:_____

_____

 CAMP

TRIP MEMORIES

WEATHER REPORT

What I Enjoyed Most:_____

_____

_____

_____

Most Memorable Event:_____

_____

_____

_____

Who I Camped With: _____

_____

People I Met: _____

_____

Places I Went: _____

_____

Things I Did: _____

_____

Things I Still Want To Try Or Do Next Time:_____

_____

_____

39 CAMPGROUND INFORMATION

CAMPGROUND:_____ DATES:_____

LOCATION:_____ SITE #:_____

PHONE:_____ NIGHTLY RATE:_____

RESERVATION #:_____

CHECK IN TIME:_____ CHECK OUT TIME:_____

POSSIBLE SITES FOR NEXT VISIT:_____

CAMPGROUND RATING: 1   2   3   4   5   6   7   8   9   10

OTHER CAMPGROUNDS IN AREA   PHONE NUMBER

_____   _____

_____   _____

☐ WATER	☐ WIFI	☐ LAKE
☐ ELECTRIC	☐ CABLE TV	☐ BEACH ACCESS
☐ SEWER	☐ POOL	☐ NATURE TRAILS
☐ TENTS OK	☐ HOT TUB	☐ CAMP STORE
☐ PULL-THROUGH	☐ PATIO	☐ FITNESS ROOM
MAX TRAILER	☐ GRILL/BBQ	☐ RESTAURANT
LENGTH_____	☐ FIRE PIT	☐ VOLLEYBALL COURT
☐ DUMP STATION	☐ SHADY TREES	☐ MINI GOLF
☐ SHOWERS	☐ PICNIC TABLES	☐ PLAYGROUND
☐ LAUNDRY	☐ BIKE RENTAL	☐ CLUB HOUSE

OTHER AMMENITIES:_____

_____

CAMP

TRIP MEMORIES

WEATHER REPORT

What I Enjoyed Most:_____

_____

_____

_____

Most Memorable Event:_____

_____

_____

_____

Who I Camped With: _____

_____

People I Met: _____

_____

Places I Went: _____

_____

Things I Did: _____

_____

Things I Still Want To Try Or Do Next Time:_____

_____

_____

40 CAMPGROUND INFORMATION

CAMPGROUND:_____ DATES:_____

LOCATION:_____ SITE #:_____

PHONE:_____ NIGHTLY RATE:_____

RESERVATION #:_____

CHECK IN TIME:_____ CHECK OUT TIME:_____

POSSIBLE SITES FOR NEXT VISIT:_____

CAMPGROUND RATING: 1   2   3   4   5   6   7   8   9   10

OTHER CAMPGROUNDS IN AREA   PHONE NUMBER

_____   _____

_____   _____

□ WATER	□ WIFI	□ LAKE
□ ELECTRIC	□ CABLE TV	□ BEACH ACCESS
□ SEWER	□ POOL	□ NATURE TRAILS
□ TENTS OK	□ HOT TUB	□ CAMP STORE
□ PULL-THROUGH	□ PATIO	□ FITNESS ROOM
MAX TRAILER	□ GRILL/BBQ	□ RESTAURANT
LENGTH_____	□ FIRE PIT	□ VOLLEYBALL COURT
□ DUMP STATION	□ SHADY TREES	□ MINI GOLF
□ SHOWERS	□ PICNIC TABLES	□ PLAYGROUND
□ LAUNDRY	□ BIKE RENTAL	□ CLUB HOUSE

OTHER AMMENITIES:_____

_____

 CAMP

TRIP MEMORIES

WEATHER REPORT

What I Enjoyed Most:_____

_____

_____

_____

Most Memorable Event:_____

_____

_____

_____

Who I Camped With: _____

_____

People I Met: _____

_____

Places I Went: _____

_____

Things I Did: _____

_____

Things I Still Want To Try Or Do Next Time:_____

_____

_____

41 CAMPGROUND INFORMATION

CAMPGROUND:_____ DATES:_____

LOCATION:_____ SITE #:_____

PHONE:_____ NIGHTLY RATE:_____

RESERVATION #:_____

CHECK IN TIME:_____ CHECK OUT TIME:_____

POSSIBLE SITES FOR NEXT VISIT:_____

CAMPGROUND RATING: 1 2 3 4 5 6 7 8 9 10

OTHER CAMPGROUNDS IN AREA   PHONE NUMBER

_____   _____

_____   _____

☐ WATER	☐ WIFI	☐ LAKE
☐ ELECTRIC	☐ CABLE TV	☐ BEACH ACCESS
☐ SEWER	☐ POOL	☐ NATURE TRAILS
☐ TENTS OK	☐ HOT TUB	☐ CAMP STORE
☐ PULL-THROUGH	☐ PATIO	☐ FITNESS ROOM
MAX TRAILER	☐ GRILL/BBQ	☐ RESTAURANT
LENGTH_____	☐ FIRE PIT	☐ VOLLEYBALL COURT
☐ DUMP STATION	☐ SHADY TREES	☐ MINI GOLF
☐ SHOWERS	☐ PICNIC TABLES	☐ PLAYGROUND
☐ LAUNDRY	☐ BIKE RENTAL	☐ CLUB HOUSE

OTHER AMMENITIES:_____

_____

 CAMP

TRIP MEMORIES

WEATHER REPORT

What I Enjoyed Most:_____

_____

_____

_____

Most Memorable Event:_____

_____

_____

_____

Who I Camped With: _____

_____

People I Met: _____

_____

Places I Went: _____

_____

Things I Did: _____

_____

Things I Still Want To Try Or Do Next Time:_____

_____

_____

42 CAMPGROUND INFORMATION

CAMPGROUND:_____ DATES:_____

LOCATION:_____ SITE #:_____

PHONE:_____ NIGHTLY RATE:_____

RESERVATION #:_____

CHECK IN TIME:_____ CHECK OUT TIME:_____

POSSIBLE SITES FOR NEXT VISIT:_____

CAMPGROUND RATING: 1 2 3 4 5 6 7 8 9 10

OTHER CAMPGROUNDS IN AREA   PHONE NUMBER

_____   _____

_____   _____

☐ WATER	☐ WIFI	☐ LAKE
☐ ELECTRIC	☐ CABLE TV	☐ BEACH ACCESS
☐ SEWER	☐ POOL	☐ NATURE TRAILS
☐ TENTS OK	☐ HOT TUB	☐ CAMP STORE
☐ PULL-THROUGH	☐ PATIO	☐ FITNESS ROOM
MAX TRAILER	☐ GRILL/BBQ	☐ RESTAURANT
LENGTH_____	☐ FIRE PIT	☐ VOLLEYBALL COURT
☐ DUMP STATION	☐ SHADY TREES	☐ MINI GOLF
☐ SHOWERS	☐ PICNIC TABLES	☐ PLAYGROUND
☐ LAUNDRY	☐ BIKE RENTAL	☐ CLUB HOUSE

OTHER AMMENITIES:_____

_____

 CAMP

TRIP MEMORIES

WEATHER REPORT

What I Enjoyed Most:_____

_____

_____

_____

Most Memorable Event:_____

_____

_____

_____

Who I Camped With: _____

_____

People I Met: _____

_____

Places I Went: _____

_____

Things I Did: _____

_____

Things I Still Want To Try Or Do Next Time:_____

_____

_____

43 CAMPGROUND INFORMATION

CAMPGROUND:_____ DATES:_____

LOCATION:_____ SITE #:_____

PHONE:_____ NIGHTLY RATE:_____

RESERVATION #:_____

CHECK IN TIME:_____ CHECK OUT TIME:_____

POSSIBLE SITES FOR NEXT VISIT:_____

CAMPGROUND RATING: 1 2 3 4 5 6 7 8 9 10

OTHER CAMPGROUNDS IN AREA   PHONE NUMBER

_____   _____

_____   _____

☐ WATER	☐ WIFI	☐ LAKE
☐ ELECTRIC	☐ CABLE TV	☐ BEACH ACCESS
☐ SEWER	☐ POOL	☐ NATURE TRAILS
☐ TENTS OK	☐ HOT TUB	☐ CAMP STORE
☐ PULL-THROUGH	☐ PATIO	☐ FITNESS ROOM
MAX TRAILER	☐ GRILL/BBQ	☐ RESTAURANT
LENGTH_____	☐ FIRE PIT	☐ VOLLEYBALL COURT
☐ DUMP STATION	☐ SHADY TREES	☐ MINI GOLF
☐ SHOWERS	☐ PICNIC TABLES	☐ PLAYGROUND
☐ LAUNDRY	☐ BIKE RENTAL	☐ CLUB HOUSE

OTHER AMMENITIES:_____

_____

 **TRIP MEMORIES**

WEATHER REPORT

What I Enjoyed Most:_____

_____

_____

_____

Most Memorable Event:_____

_____

_____

_____

Who I Camped With: _____

_____

People I Met: _____

_____

Places I Went: _____

_____

Things I Did: _____

_____

Things I Still Want To Try Or Do Next Time:_____

_____

_____

44 CAMPGROUND INFORMATION

CAMPGROUND:_____ DATES:_____

LOCATION:_____ SITE #:_____

PHONE:_____ NIGHTLY RATE:_____

RESERVATION #:_____

CHECK IN TIME:_____ CHECK OUT TIME:_____

POSSIBLE SITES FOR NEXT VISIT:_____

CAMPGROUND RATING: 1   2   3   4   5   6   7   8   9   10

OTHER CAMPGROUNDS IN AREA   PHONE NUMBER

_____   _____

_____   _____

□ WATER	□ WIFI	□ LAKE
□ ELECTRIC	□ CABLE TV	□ BEACH ACCESS
□ SEWER	□ POOL	□ NATURE TRAILS
□ TENTS OK	□ HOT TUB	□ CAMP STORE
□ PULL-THROUGH	□ PATIO	□ FITNESS ROOM
MAX TRAILER	□ GRILL/BBQ	□ RESTAURANT
LENGTH_____	□ FIRE PIT	□ VOLLEYBALL COURT
□ DUMP STATION	□ SHADY TREES	□ MINI GOLF
□ SHOWERS	□ PICNIC TABLES	□ PLAYGROUND
□ LAUNDRY	□ BIKE RENTAL	□ CLUB HOUSE

OTHER AMMENITIES:_____

_____

CAMP

TRIP MEMORIES

WEATHER REPORT

What I Enjoyed Most:_____

_____

_____

_____

Most Memorable Event:_____

_____

_____

_____

Who I Camped With: _____

_____

People I Met: _____

_____

Places I Went: _____

_____

Things I Did: _____

_____

Things I Still Want To Try Or Do Next Time:_____

_____

_____

45  CAMPGROUND INFORMATION

CAMPGROUND:_____ DATES:_____

LOCATION:_____ SITE #:_____

PHONE:_____ NIGHTLY RATE:_____

RESERVATION #:_____

CHECK IN TIME:_____ CHECK OUT TIME:_____

POSSIBLE SITES FOR NEXT VISIT:_____

CAMPGROUND RATING: 1 2 3 4 5 6 7 8 9 10

OTHER CAMPGROUNDS IN AREA   PHONE NUMBER

_____   _____

_____   _____

□ WATER	□ WIFI	□ LAKE
□ ELECTRIC	□ CABLE TV	□ BEACH ACCESS
□ SEWER	□ POOL	□ NATURE TRAILS
□ TENTS OK	□ HOT TUB	□ CAMP STORE
□ PULL-THROUGH	□ PATIO	□ FITNESS ROOM
MAX TRAILER	□ GRILL/BBQ	□ RESTAURANT
LENGTH_____	□ FIRE PIT	□ VOLLEYBALL COURT
□ DUMP STATION	□ SHADY TREES	□ MINI GOLF
□ SHOWERS	□ PICNIC TABLES	□ PLAYGROUND
□ LAUNDRY	□ BIKE RENTAL	□ CLUB HOUSE

OTHER AMMENITIES:_____

_____

CAMP

TRIP MEMORIES

WEATHER REPORT

What I Enjoyed Most: _____

_____

_____

_____

Most Memorable Event: _____

_____

_____

_____

Who I Camped With: _____

_____

People I Met: _____

_____

Places I Went: _____

_____

Things I Did: _____

_____

Things I Still Want To Try Or Do Next Time: _____

_____

_____

46  CAMPGROUND INFORMATION

CAMPGROUND:_____ DATES:_____

LOCATION:_____ SITE #:_____

PHONE:_____ NIGHTLY RATE:_____

RESERVATION #:_____

CHECK IN TIME:_____ CHECK OUT TIME:_____

POSSIBLE SITES FOR NEXT VISIT:_____

CAMPGROUND RATING: 1   2   3   4   5   6   7   8   9   10

OTHER CAMPGROUNDS IN AREA   PHONE NUMBER

_____   _____

_____   _____

☐ WATER	☐ WIFI	☐ LAKE
☐ ELECTRIC	☐ CABLE TV	☐ BEACH ACCESS
☐ SEWER	☐ POOL	☐ NATURE TRAILS
☐ TENTS OK	☐ HOT TUB	☐ CAMP STORE
☐ PULL-THROUGH	☐ PATIO	☐ FITNESS ROOM
MAX TRAILER	☐ GRILL/BBQ	☐ RESTAURANT
LENGTH_____	☐ FIRE PIT	☐ VOLLEYBALL COURT
☐ DUMP STATION	☐ SHADY TREES	☐ MINI GOLF
☐ SHOWERS	☐ PICNIC TABLES	☐ PLAYGROUND
☐ LAUNDRY	☐ BIKE RENTAL	☐ CLUB HOUSE

OTHER AMMENITIES:_____

_____

 **CAMP**

TRIP MEMORIES

WEATHER REPORT

What I Enjoyed Most:_____

_____

_____

_____

Most Memorable Event:_____

_____

_____

_____

Who I Camped With: _____

_____

People I Met: _____

_____

Places I Went: _____

_____

Things I Did: _____

_____

Things I Still Want To Try Or Do Next Time:_____

_____

_____

47  CAMPGROUND INFORMATION

CAMPGROUND:_____ DATES:_____

LOCATION:_____ SITE #:_____

PHONE:_____ NIGHTLY RATE:_____

RESERVATION #:_____

CHECK IN TIME:_____ CHECK OUT TIME:_____

POSSIBLE SITES FOR NEXT VISIT:_____

CAMPGROUND RATING: 1 2 3 4 5 6 7 8 9 10

OTHER CAMPGROUNDS IN AREA   PHONE NUMBER

_____   _____

_____   _____

□ WATER	□ WIFI	□ LAKE
□ ELECTRIC	□ CABLE TV	□ BEACH ACCESS
□ SEWER	□ POOL	□ NATURE TRAILS
□ TENTS OK	□ HOT TUB	□ CAMP STORE
□ PULL-THROUGH	□ PATIO	□ FITNESS ROOM
MAX TRAILER	□ GRILL/BBQ	□ RESTAURANT
LENGTH_____	□ FIRE PIT	□ VOLLEYBALL COURT
□ DUMP STATION	□ SHADY TREES	□ MINI GOLF
□ SHOWERS	□ PICNIC TABLES	□ PLAYGROUND
□ LAUNDRY	□ BIKE RENTAL	□ CLUB HOUSE

OTHER AMMENITIES:_____

_____

CAMP

TRIP MEMORIES

WEATHER REPORT

What I Enjoyed Most:_____

_____

_____

_____

Most Memorable Event:_____

_____

_____

_____

Who I Camped With: _____

_____

People I Met: _____

_____

Places I Went: _____

_____

Things I Did: _____

_____

Things I Still Want To Try Or Do Next Time:_____

_____

_____

48 CAMPGROUND INFORMATION

CAMPGROUND:_____ DATES:_____

LOCATION:_____ SITE #:_____

PHONE:_____ NIGHTLY RATE:_____

RESERVATION #:_____

CHECK IN TIME:_____ CHECK OUT TIME:_____

POSSIBLE SITES FOR NEXT VISIT:_____

CAMPGROUND RATING: 1   2   3   4   5   6   7   8   9   10

OTHER CAMPGROUNDS IN AREA   PHONE NUMBER

_____   _____

_____   _____

☐ WATER	☐ WIFI	☐ LAKE
☐ ELECTRIC	☐ CABLE TV	☐ BEACH ACCESS
☐ SEWER	☐ POOL	☐ NATURE TRAILS
☐ TENTS OK	☐ HOT TUB	☐ CAMP STORE
☐ PULL-THROUGH	☐ PATIO	☐ FITNESS ROOM
MAX TRAILER	☐ GRILL/BBQ	☐ RESTAURANT
LENGTH_____	☐ FIRE PIT	☐ VOLLEYBALL COURT
☐ DUMP STATION	☐ SHADY TREES	☐ MINI GOLF
☐ SHOWERS	☐ PICNIC TABLES	☐ PLAYGROUND
☐ LAUNDRY	☐ BIKE RENTAL	☐ CLUB HOUSE

OTHER AMMENITIES:_____

_____

 CAMP

TRIP MEMORIES

WEATHER REPORT

What I Enjoyed Most:_____

_____

.

_____

_____

Most Memorable Event:_____

_____

_____

_____

Who I Camped With: _____

_____

People I Met: _____

_____

Places I Went: _____

_____

Things I Did: _____

_____

Things I Still Want To Try Or Do Next Time:_____

_____

_____

49 CAMPGROUND INFORMATION

CAMPGROUND:_____ DATES:_____

LOCATION:_____ SITE #:_____

PHONE:_____ NIGHTLY RATE:_____

RESERVATION #:_____

CHECK IN TIME:_____ CHECK OUT TIME:_____

POSSIBLE SITES FOR NEXT VISIT:_____

CAMPGROUND RATING: 1 2 3 4 5 6 7 8 9 10

OTHER CAMPGROUNDS IN AREA   PHONE NUMBER

_____   _____

_____   _____

☐ WATER	☐ WIFI	☐ LAKE
☐ ELECTRIC	☐ CABLE TV	☐ BEACH ACCESS
☐ SEWER	☐ POOL	☐ NATURE TRAILS
☐ TENTS OK	☐ HOT TUB	☐ CAMP STORE
☐ PULL-THROUGH	☐ PATIO	☐ FITNESS ROOM
MAX TRAILER	☐ GRILL/BBQ	☐ RESTAURANT
LENGTH_____	☐ FIRE PIT	☐ VOLLEYBALL COURT
☐ DUMP STATION	☐ SHADY TREES	☐ MINI GOLF
☐ SHOWERS	☐ PICNIC TABLES	☐ PLAYGROUND
☐ LAUNDRY	☐ BIKE RENTAL	☐ CLUB HOUSE

OTHER AMMENITIES:_____

_____

CAMP

TRIP MEMORIES

WEATHER REPORT

What I Enjoyed Most:_____

_____

_____

_____

Most Memorable Event:_____

_____

_____

_____

Who I Camped With: _____

_____

People I Met: _____

_____

Places I Went: _____

_____

Things I Did: _____

_____

Things I Still Want To Try Or Do Next Time:_____

_____

_____

50 CAMPGROUND INFORMATION

CAMPGROUND:_____ DATES:_____

LOCATION:_____ SITE #:_____

PHONE:_____ NIGHTLY RATE:_____

RESERVATION #:_____

CHECK IN TIME:_____ CHECK OUT TIME:_____

POSSIBLE SITES FOR NEXT VISIT:_____

CAMPGROUND RATING: 1 2 3 4 5 6 7 8 9 10

OTHER CAMPGROUNDS IN AREA   PHONE NUMBER

_____   _____

_____   _____

☐ WATER	☐ WIFI	☐ LAKE
☐ ELECTRIC	☐ CABLE TV	☐ BEACH ACCESS
☐ SEWER	☐ POOL	☐ NATURE TRAILS
☐ TENTS OK	☐ HOT TUB	☐ CAMP STORE
☐ PULL-THROUGH	☐ PATIO	☐ FITNESS ROOM
MAX TRAILER	☐ GRILL/BBQ	☐ RESTAURANT
LENGTH_____	☐ FIRE PIT	☐ VOLLEYBALL COURT
☐ DUMP STATION	☐ SHADY TREES	☐ MINI GOLF
☐ SHOWERS	☐ PICNIC TABLES	☐ PLAYGROUND
☐ LAUNDRY	☐ BIKE RENTAL	☐ CLUB HOUSE

OTHER AMMENITIES:_____

_____

CAMP TRIP MEMORIES

WEATHER REPORT

What I Enjoyed Most:_____

_____

_____

_____

Most Memorable Event:_____

_____

_____

_____

Who I Camped With: _____

_____

People I Met: _____

_____

Places I Went: _____

_____

Things I Did: _____

_____

Things I Still Want To Try Or Do Next Time:_____

_____

_____

Made in the USA
Columbia, SC
27 July 2019